The Way of Power

poems by Red Hawk

ORA LABORA
(to Work is to pray)

HOHM PRESS, Prescott, Arizona 86302

Acknowledgements

The following poems appeared first in these magazines:

Tawagoto: What the Spiritual Master Said, Entering Reality, the Difference Between Art and Business;

The Arkansas Arts Chronicle: Me and Ginsburg Read in Hot Springs, Small Breasted Women, What Has Become of the Tenured Professors.

The New York Quarterly: Bulletin: Red Hawk is Not a Real Indian.

Cover art by Gary Simmons, portrait artist
133 Brown Dr., Hot Springs, AR 71913

Much of this book was completed as the Alfred Hodder Fellow in the Humanities at Princeton University; my sincere thanks for their kindness and generosity.

ISBN 0-934252-64-5

Library of Congress card number 96-075395

Hohm Press
P.O. Box 2501
Prescott, AZ 86302
520-778-9189
Fax 520-717-1779

Contents

This book is for my Gurus:

Little Wind & Rain Drop;
Osho (Grandfather);
Oyate Shunkawakan Waste (Good Horse Nation);
Mister J;
Mister Lee, Khēpa Baul (the Good Father);
Andre Enard (Teacher of Dancing);
Barbara Bishop;
Gayle Maxine;
Tom and Joanna;
Mary Louise;
Don Juan Matus.

Prologue: The Way of Power

The Way of Power

I will tell you how it is with Power.
The Way is hard
and easily lost.

Take me for example.
Once I had a tiny power
no greater than the breath of a bird,
the power to make words.
But it was more than I could handle.

I was sloppy with it,
spoke too much
and at the wrong times,
used the poems badly
for my own glory.

So the Power was taken away.
Even the breath of a bird
made me vain and arrogant
and I used it to make myself little.

Now I sit still on my porch
and I see how
I am a stupid man
who was made sick
by the bird's breath.

I am dying of it
because the breath got inside me
before I made myself strong
and now it is blowing me away
like a small frail bird
caught in a high wind.

What is left for me
is to die quietly
because my stupidity made a big noise.
This is what I know
about Power.

part i: How Power Corrupts

The Wild Dog

Mind resists the orderly,
thinks freedom is in thinking
any thought it wishes.

Like a wild dog who has felt the whip,
the mind snarls
at the hand that tames it, resists

the collar of Attention, strains
at the leash of meditation, claws
and runs to avoid discipline.

A wild dog can be tamed by the whip
but it will turn on you and
at the first chance, run for it;

it will never be good company.
It may hunt but
it will mangle the bird.

Better the dog who by gentle patience
is shown the way over and over.
That dog will one day lick your hand,

will be devoted to you and serve
at quiet command, will lay down
its life at your feet

and when it fetches the bird
no feather will be ruffled,
no toothmark upon the flesh.

The Champions Are Dead

We live in an age when
the dim souls are ascending to
the highest offices, they are
becoming the rulers and this is
what the Sages call a Dark Age.
The worst thing you can have
in a time like this is real talent.
The first thing the dim souls do
when they get power is ferret out
those who shine and they
line them up along a wall
and shoot them.
But they always save one for a trial,
put it on TV so everyone can see and
when the conviction comes down they
hang him in public where it will be
seen and known what is acceptable
and what cannot be allowed.
Once the champions are dead
you get an age like ours which the Sages
call a Dark Age, where the poets
are official and speak in the voice
of their masters and when their masters
are universities and the universities are
owned by the state and the state is run
by the dim souls who have ascended to
the highest offices then you have
what the Sages call a Dark Age
and woe, woe unto you whose
light shines brightly for you
will be persecuted and your
brief candle extinguished.

Richard Nixon's Funeral

The dirty scheming little crook is dead
and they are lined up before the cameras
to praise him, who once villified him.
He got his start by telling vicious lies

about Helen Douglas, a good woman,
hinting she was a communist, and he
never stopped as long as he lived.
A corrupt contemptible coward,

a darkly paranoid madman, a consort
of Joe McCarthy's and Roy Cohn's, he
lied his way to the highest offices and now
they can't say enough about him.

The funeral motorcade is blocks long.
There is a law in politics:
the greater the fool,
the longer the motorcade

and the deeper they shovel the praise.

What They Did To Sitting Bull

Lured into the fort by the promise
of meat for his people, they meant to
murder him for the Ghost Dance
and because he was a power they
could not understand or tame,
so they did.
Murder him.
They shot and shot him until
he fell in the snow like a sack
of wet corn meal and the blood
ran out of him like the cry
of a lone Crow in an empty sky.

Then they quartered the body,
hacked it into 4 pieces
with an axe,
thinking this would keep him
from coming back and put an end
to his power.
Because they had no understanding,
they could not know
it increased his power 4 times,
sent him in the 4 directions and
opened 4 doors into the starry worlds.
You can fool a starving dog with

the promise of meat, but
a man of real power will
eat your heart and relish
every lie and frail conceit;
he will feast on your weakness
and for every one you kill,
4 will come seeking your unborn children
and they will carve them from your loins and
they will carry them away
and feed them to the ravenous Crow
who waits there in the empty sky
for the meat which was promised him.

Charles Bukowski is Dead at 73

This is the part Hank would have loved best,
when all the critics lie down
on their beds of nails, bemoaning
the passing of a bum
who had a way with words.

Stand! Stand! A poet has died
and he was the rarest kind:
he told the truth about himself.
Most of them hide behind the poem
but Hank stood and exposed himself
to fire.
He was no liar.

Stand! Stand! A poet passed this way
and now has passed away.
Long after the others of his age
went silent and gave up, he was
still in a bad mood, drunk and raging
against the dying of the light
and now the bum is dead.

Stand! Stand! A bum has died,
a voice is still that once did tell the truth
when all around him lied.
In a dark age that does not love the poem,
give us courage to stand and sing
when we would run and hide.
Give us the necessary pride
to tell the truth though we are weak.
God have mercy on those of us
who are left to speak.

Photograph of the Indians Signing Over Their Land, 1950

Same picture you see in all the history books,
the chief signs, surrounded by soldiers, then
some general sits down to sign. Only now
the chief is surrounded by men in suits,

and some fat white bureaucrat with no name
signs the paper.
George Gillette is chief of the Hidatsu tribe
and he has just signed over to them

the frontage land along the Missouri River
they will need for the Garrison Dam project,
land the Hidatsu and Mandan have lived on
for more than a thousand years.

He has broken down weeping as they
take the photo, his face in one hand,
his glasses dangling from the other like
a broken and useless promise.

His suit does not fit, his weeping
has created an empty space around him
3 or 4 feet wide, like the space
the living make around someone dying.

Not a single white man in the room
is looking at George Gillette.
They are, every one of them,
looking at the fat bureaucrat

signing the paper.
It is the only way they can do it
and not feel a thing; it is
the way they've always done it:

pretend the son-of-a-bitch
is not there.

I Break All the Rules at Ben Franklin Elementary

I am talking to a hundred of them
about death, God and the Indians
when one of them farts loudly

and time stops;
the silence and the stink hang there.
All of the scoldings and whippings

and public humiliations are not enough
to stifle the low wave of giggles
and then I say, Who farted?

All hell breaks loose.
The teachers are lined up along one wall;
their faces freeze over.

The principal rises, her jaw set like iron pipe.
Jeffrey, she intones in an icy rage,
you go wait in my office. NOW.

The little boy rises from the sacred circle
I have so carefully made. No, I say,
able to save only one face, hers or his.

I put my arm around him and sit him
up front, next to me. When I am done
she comes up to me with a look that

would bring God to heel.
3 things you never do in a school,
she says handing me my $50 check,

Talk about God or death
or violate a teacher's authority.
I give her back the check,

which stops her in mid-reprimand.
She seems pleased and dumbfounded.
As I walk to my car, the students along

one side of the building bang the windows
and wave to me. They do not know
I have just purchased Jeffrey's redemption,

all they know is that here is a man
who laughs at farts and
does not like the principal.

The Failure of the Poets

In my time they have not understood
where the traps were.
Maybe they have never understood this
but in my time they were ruined by
the universities and the proliferation
ot grants, the lecture circuit and the
prize money competitions. And always
too many goddamned anthologies.

But the universities were the worst because
once they take that much money and have
that much time and see all the fine young
girls who want to get to know them, it is
too late.
They will do whatever they are told
and say what they are allowed to say
because it is too easy.

And then they start to sound alike.
They hide behind the poem and they
have to publish more books for their
tenure and once they worry about the
number of books, there is no more poet.
All there is then is another accountant
inflating the language to achieve the numbers.
In my time there has been a failure of nerve,

the poets have feared going it alone.
In the old days it used to be that
once poets lost their nerve then they
joined the long lists: they jumped off of boats
into the propeller, they jumped off bridges
onto the ice, they stuck their heads in the ovens.
In my time they get tenure and they go
without a struggle into the committee rooms.

The Day I Went Before the Tenure Committee

There are 4 of them, 2 men,
2 women. One woman is old and sour;
all the lines around her mouth
turn down. The other

is younger and has lost her man
to another woman. She is
the first to speak.
We have reports you are

hugging your students in class,
she says and they all stare at me.
I admit it.
One of the men is silver haired

and smooth. He was fired
by the woman who hired me and his friends
revolted, got her sacked, brought him
back the year I came. He looks

at me and smiles. We both know
there is not room enough for the 2 of us
on the same planet.
There is no room, he says,

for physical displays in the classroom.
The classroom is not the place for love,
the young woman says and they all sit there
nodding and staring at me.

I know I am finished
but it is a splendid moment,
one of those rare moments
when everyone comes out of hiding

and shows themselves
for what they are.
Sometimes,
that has to be enough.

What Has Become of the Tenured Professors

When I was young and fresh in the university
the thing I did not expect was the cynicism, the
cheap cruel pettiness of the tenured elite and
I was not prepared to defend myself so
they ripped me to pieces.

One was an arrogant insufferable woman
who left her husband for a scientist
whose marriage was a wreck. They have
been together 17 years and he's had 3 heart attacks.
She changes his dirty underwear and when she

comes into the place where I work she looks tired,
all the arrogance beaten out of her.
Then there is the
handsome man with the beautiful wife.
He got tenure and I did not see him for 15 years.

Last week we met in a grocery store and I see he is
on the kind of medication they give to those who
have lost it altogether and cannot find their way
back from the edge. He is desperate to talk,
traps me and pours it all out in a frenzy:

one daughter was a suicide, the other is hopelessly mad,
and a brave loyal wife whose beauty was fed
to the lions of sorrow, who can never be satisfied.
Tenure does not keep the demons from the door
nor the terror from the heart; it does not

save the children of the damned
from clawing at their frail breasts, nor
ease the grief of the world for a single moment.
No one gets tenure here.
We suffer our brief occasional joy

and then we die.
Tenure is a bone thrown to
arrogant fools who believe that
now somehow, they will be
saved from the anguish.

Horseshit Harry

He was at the track every day
and he always had a hot tip.
You could count on Harry;
if he tipped you on a horse
it was sure to lose.
After the crowds had gone home
you could always find Harry
going through the tickets on the ground,
hoping he would finally
find a winner.

So today I read in the paper that
Harry's wife was convicted for his murder.
Seems she put poison in his food
every day until it killed him
and they caught her.

Harry never could pick 'em
worth a damn.

Bearing the Wound of Wisdom

Once when I was a boy,
my friend Huff and I made slingshots
and hunted in the woods along the tracks
where we came upon a small rabbit
frozen in place and trying to hide.

Huff hit him with a lucky shot
thud! right in the ribs and it
knocked the rabbit over
so it lay there stunned.
Huff says, Now we gotta kill him,

and I say, no no don't.
But he thumps stone after stone
into its ribs until it is dead
and something precious in me breaks
like the mainspring in a fine watch;

once it goes, time stops
and the heart grows silent,
its tick-tock muted by the blows
of those who know nothing
and suppose they are wise.

Wisdom cuts to the bone;
its seed is sewn in ignorance
when the cost is unknown to us,
then the long labor done alone
to pay, to tend, to atone.

I Believe in a Simple Violence

Like this poem.
For years the poems have borne the weight
of my rage, my proclivity to violence.
It is far better than the bullet to the brain
which is too quick, or the knife
to the gut which hurts bad for awhile
but you could recover.
No, the word on the page is how I like it.
It lingers,
it keeps the wound always open,
it makes the bastards squirm.

That is how us petty tyrants operate.
Revenge is not enough if
torture is possible.
We don't just like to pin them
to the board, we
like to watch them wriggle.

The fist is crude,
weapons messy. There is
something clean and simple
about the word. It kills
but they go on living and
they never forget it is always
still there where

anyone can pick it up and
pull the trigger
again.

In the Trees at the Edge of the Madhouse

There is no fence so
you do not want to go too far
onto the property for fear
they will find you out
and believe you are one of them.
The first naked woman I ever saw
was in those trees when I was 15.
She was the whitest woman I've ever seen
so the thick black richness of her
body hair was a shock like the time
I saw a black dog frozen face down
in the new snow, its legs spread out
to the sides like her arms as she
turned round and round in one spot,
first the black triangle against the snow
of her flesh, then the lush buttocks cleavage.
Men in white jackets came for her and
they were rough, their cruel hands grabbing
and squeezing at the hair until she screamed
at the very same time I did and they
all froze there looking at me until
one of them came after me while the other
yelled, He's one of ours. Get him.
But he could not catch me in the trees.
Every time we drove by the madhouse
my drunken father used to say,
Not all the loonies is inside,
and not all that's inside is loonies.
He should know;
he was one of them
and I was not.
I was one who got away.

You Know What You Are, Buddy

As I am pulling into the gas station
a woman roars out from behind a pump
and cuts right in front of me.
I slam on the brakes, lay on my horn

and she stops just long enough to
lean out her window and scream at me,
You know what you are, buddy.
Yeah.   I do.

I am a sorry little loser who
doesn't know his ass from a gas pump;
I am an arrogant educated skreed who
will show you everything I know for a dollar;

I am a scared tense lonely humbug
willing to sell myself to the first woman
who shows me a grain of kindness;
I am a dazed and hopeless idiot

wondering how I got here and what
I am going to do next; I am a third-rate poet,
a broken and ruined lover of God,
a spiritual derelict hooked on Dharma,

a bum for truth, a pimp
for the teachings of Masters, but
what I want to know is,
how could she tell?

part ii: The Way of Adoration and Devotion

Guru
women
children
Earth

Guru

What the Spiritual Master Said

I am a worthless sinner, a
dirty beggar, a fool
He said and
everyone thought
how humble, how
perfectly modest and beautiful.
What we could not imagine, because
we did not yet know ourselves well,
was that He had no choice;
He had to tell the whole truth
about Himself exactly like He saw it
from the inside where nothing
was hidden, nothing
gilded or made to smell nice.

But here is the beauty of it.
He who knew He was a dirty beggar,
and confessed it without pride or loathing,
shone
with a radiance so bright that
all we who stood near to Him were
compelled to bow down at His feet
and adore Him. We could not
do otherwise.

Nothing
shines so brightly
as the man who knows Himself
and without show or bitterness
places Himself on the bottom rung
that others may stand on His shoulders
and reach for the Sun;

He is greater
than a thousand kings.

The Difference Between Art and Business
(for Mister Lee)

Mister Lee taught me that the struggle for the Soul
is not art; it is
all Business.
Art can sustain great losses, forever.

But where the Soul is concerned
the Guru can only carry a person so long and then
He has to cut His losses,   ruthlessly.
You will be left wandering and alone

like that poor bastard Ouspensky;
one of the great geniuses, he found
a Spiritual Master named Gurdjieff and wrote
the definitive book on his Master's ideas,

a real work of art.
Gurdjieff proceeded to kick his ass inside out.
Ouspensky, being a great logician, thought
he had everything figured out,   everything.

But he could not keep up with Gurdjieff,
who was crazy and wise; Ouspensky
would not bear the seed of Ignorance
even for his Master. So one day

Gurdjieff told him never to return.
Years later when he had been drinking heavily
Ouspensky sat in a room weeping.
    Why does He not send for me,

he asked over and over about his Guru:
because he paid for the teaching but
when he was called upon for it,
he would not fork over the Interest.

The Good Apprentice

He did what he was told
with complete attention.

The others didn't like him;
there were always a dozen or so.
They came and they went,
but he stayed on
doing his Master's work.

Slowly he changed,
but he was in no hurry.
He grew still
and it made the others curious.
They wondered if he had powers.
He said he had no powers.
They didn't believe him.

He did what he was told.
He paid attention.
He grew simple and slow
and it made the others envious.
They wondered if he knew the Master's secrets.
He said he had no secrets.
They didn't like him
because he would not tell the secrets.

One day the Master called him.
They were together a short time.
The next day he was gone.
Just like that.

It made the others fearful.
one or two
began to do what they were told.
They began to pay attention.
The others didn't like that.
They came and they went.
One or two stayed on.

This is My Body, Eat of Me

I am riding with the beautiful Guru
and some of His disciples.
They won't let Him alone.
The new band drummer is 17, He says.
No Baba, he's 18
one of them argues. Or
is he 17. She can't decide.
Baba, did you like the dinner
another one asks.
Turn here, Baba. No, I'm wrong
turn at the next street,
a third one directs. And it
goes on like this without ceasing.

He does not argue. He
does not yell or curse. But
it wears at Him, it
consumes Him crumb by
remorseless crumb.
I do not know what I can possibly do.
Maybe this is what it means to be a Master,
that you lay down your body
on an anthill and you
do not scream.

The Guru is consumed.
It is inevitable, relentless.
Even those who know better
cannot help themselves.
I turn to Him, teeth bared,
eager for my fill
before it is
all gone.

Entering Reality

We are going to the home of the Spiritual Master
having flown 1,000 miles
and driven an hour and a half
because there is nothing in this world for me
like beholding the wonder of His face.

As we enter the gates of the Ashram
I am reminded of what a pilot once told me:
there is a point when an airplane is
¼ mile out from the end of the runway,
150 feet off the ground, 200 m.p.h.

when no matter what occurs
it cannot go back on its landing;
they call this,   entering reality.
We approach the house and see Mister Lee
sitting there in His chair waiting.

As we reach the sliding glass doors
He looks up, smiling, eyes
like 2 planets consumed with glory.
We enter.
There is no going back.

The Nicest Man I Ever Met

I am a hopeless idiot.

Mister Lee knows this and
He does not condemn me for it because
He is the nicest man I ever met.
Instead, He asks me to do small things
which even I can do:
write me a book review,

hold the flashlight,
tell me when it is 7 o'clock,
write me a poem.
I feel good doing these for the Guru,
my Lord and Father, because He is
the nicest man I ever met.

He smiles and embraces his
hopeless idiot. That is His way
of blessing and giving me courage.
He knows what I need
and have no hope of ever getting.
He lets me ride in His van and

sit beside His desk. He comforts me
even when I am an idiot in public.
There are advantages to no hope:
I need to impress no one and
I can adore my Lord and Father
openly and without shame

because He is the nicest man
and He has a weakness
for the stupid and crazy.
He cannot resist hugging us.
Without our darkness,
how would His Light shine.

Tutwalla Baba

When he died at 93
by all reports he looked 30,
face unlined, dark hair down
to the ground, radiant and beautiful.

His spiritual practice was simple:
he walked with his eyes
downcast,
rarely spoke.

When he looked people in the eye
it burned them alive and
when he spoke
it broke them.

Refusing to be a liar,
Baba stepped into the holy fire;
reticence and restraint
made him a saint.

The Master Thief

Father, teach me your art,
his youngest son begged.
So one night they went to the palace,
pried a window, and slipped inside.

Soundlessly he moved in the dark
as if he lived there, his son close behind.
They came to a great mahogany cabinet.
    Quickly, inside!   he hissed.

    Take anything of value.
So the young man climbed in.
The old man locked the door.
    Thief, thief!   he shrieked,

smashed a vase against the wall
and escaped through the window.
All the servants came with candles;
one maid stood near the cabinet.

She heard a sound like a cat mewing,
and when she opened the door
something blew out her candle,
brushed past her and out the window.

An hour later, in a rage,
the son burst into his father's room.
    You are a monster, he seethed.
    I have barely escaped with my life.

The old man rubbed sleep from his eyes.
    What, you are alive? he said. Good.
    Then you have learned the art.
And he went back to sleep.

women

Adoro Te Devote
(Sweet Apple)

She is up before me, feeding them,
dishing oats into their buckets,
holding their muzzles as they nose her,
rub their heads against her;
they adore her.

She moves into the garden
like a dawn horse in a dewy field,
touches and murmurs to the Earth
as it bends before her devotion;
with a pause and a soft bow
she takes 2 apples from the tree.

The animals move to touch her again
as she cuts through the barn
reaching for them, their bodies
radiant in the morning light.
She cuts one apple:
half to the mare,
half to the foal.

When I come in for breakfast
the other apple is sliced neatly on my plate,
the bowl steams with oatmeal.
Woman   beautiful woman,
oh how the animals adore you.

Small Breasted Women

One thing you know for sure about them:
they have resisted the tyranny of fashion;
they have not given their breasts
to the men with knives.

The small breast is a delicate sufficiency,
a pleasing sliver of beauty
like the quarter moon in a clear sky;
like the Grace of God it is

so lovely it can be taken only
in small doses.
The Soul, driven from heaven,
still longs for the gentle curve

recalling the arc of its lost wings.
It is as simple as this:
he who comes to the breast empty handed
as if he were praying

will be full in the heart;
who comes greedy like a cheat coveting coins
will be left forever wanting.
Real sorrow is the failure

to adore what is.

One Definition of Devotion

My sister Joy was fat. She lied,
she stole, she cussed, she screwed, she
drank, she ate too much candy,
she played hooky, she went with bad boys
in their fast cars, and she fought my father

who was a mean ruthless tyrannical drunk.
She fought him at the top of her voice, with her
wits and her will and when all of that failed
she fought him on the front lawn with her fists.
If she had had a gun she would have

shot the bastard but it is good she didn't;
he died alone and insane, his gut eaten by cancer
and he got exactly what he deserved.
We all do. You can talk about your
pretty and your nice girls but

I will take my sister every time. Her will
made her stand out from the crowd; not
one more pretty face, she took no shit and
she refused to be a nice girl in a mean world.
There are so many ways to sound

the depth of a woman's devotion.
My sister's was the kind you see
in Saint Joan when they burned her alive:
she would not yield and
she could not be bought.

Cirrhosis of the Liver

My mother weighed 83 pounds when she died
and she did not know who I was. 40 years
of cheap wine every day took it all
from her, every last living decent thing
and it
put her in diapers on a machine that
sucked the snot out of her throat so
she could go on suffering a bit longer
and when finally they asked me
if they should fire the machine up again
I shook my head NO
and held her while she died.

I held my heart in my arms in that
cheap empty pitiless nursing home room
not another person who had ever known her
anywhere around and I watched her
strangle, watched
her shut down the most hopeless life
I have ever seen and when finally
even she had enough she looked
straight at me and smiled and left.
I walked out of there prepared for almost nothing
but I knew for sure that there are
a whole lot of things in this life

worse than dying
and that is not such a bad thing
to have gotten from one's mother.

Jackson Pollock's Ugly Widow

Those who make it their business
to know such things say she was
the shrewdest art dealer who ever lived,
in 20 years increasing the value of the estate
from 80 thousand to 50 million
by refusing and refusing and

refusing to sell.
One of those guys who made it
his business to know said there were
3 great art dealers in our time:
Castelli, Matisse, and the widow.
What few people ever understood,

because there are so few able to
understand something like this,
was that she might have held on
to the paintings because she
loved them and couldn't bear to
let them go.

She said as much and I believe her.
By all accounts an ugly woman,
still it is hard not to see her as
something rare and even beautiful:
she stayed to the end with a
bad mean crazy drunk,

cared for him when he was
worth less than nothing and then
when he died a bad drunk's death,
thrown from his car headfirst
into a tree and the millions piled up
like dead bodies on a dangerous curve,

she would not sell because she
loved them more than money. People
who make it their business to know
such things say it is a wise man who
marries an ugly woman because she
will be true to him until the end.

I don't know about such things but
if the widow can take a rude beast
like Pollock who poured it straight
from the can onto the floor because
it was the only way he could do it
and she can make him look wise,

who is the greater artist,
and by what crude standard
do we judge a woman's beauty,
by what frail reason do we
weigh the labors of a person's heart,
call one wifery and the other art.

Snow Falls

Debbie Snow had the voice of an angel,
the best I ever heard;
the kind that takes the human word,
lifts it from the mouths of beasts

and holds it up to God, who rings it
like a chime in the empty heart
so as she sings something is healed,
something wounded beyond repair.

Well, she died today and the sorrow
falls in my heart like a heavy snow.
How I hate to see her go away.
We wrote the songs together, Snow and me.

She did the music, me the words
and I tell you that even the worst thing
I ever wrote made me weep in disbelief
when it came out of her mouth

she was so good, her voice such a relief
in a world like this where you can search
your whole life for something real
to feed your heart and never be satisfied.

She satisfied me; I think they will have her play
on the far side of the river of death,
her golden hair falling like a blizzard of light
as she calls to the dead souls, easing them,

singing them over the water like
snow geese over a pale pond
ringing with moonlight. She will sing
until the last sentient being has crossed.

When they have all been fed, then
Snow will fall at the feet of God.
When your time comes to leave the body
and you reach the edge of the dark river

look for the light shining from her hair,
listen for her voice: it will ring
like a chime in your heart; it will satisfy;
it will sing you across the river of death.

Real Love

The blonde in the next booth is pissed.
Don't come near me, she curses her boyfriend
who has changed seats to sit beside her.
If you really loved me
you would never look at other women.

You don't know what real love is, he says
and I am reminded of Ma Amritananda Mayi
who is meditating with her disciples
in the temple one day when a leper
comes to her gate begging to see her.

His sores are oozing, his stumps raw
and bleeding, his stink so bad
you can smell him 30 feet away.
Her senior disciples refuse to let him in
thinking they would rather die

than let something like that
come into contact with their Guru,
whom they really love.
So he beings to yell and weep,
crying out for them to let him see her.

In the temple Ma hears the noise
and when she finds out what is going on
she sends for the leper at once.
When he comes, her disciples back away
but Ma goes right up to him

and peels off his rags.
She licks his open sores
and her disciples go crazy,
knocking each other over to get away,
retching and crying out in horror.

In 3 weeks his sores are gone
and his stumps healed over.
The hell I don't asshole,
the blonde says to her boyfriend and
storms out of the restaurant in a rage.

children

My Beautiful Child
(for the Wind & the Rain)

How soon the autumn has come for me
when yesterday it was summer and you
slept on the porch with me and we woke
with tickles and sang our good morning
to the merry Sunshine.

Oh my beautiful child how the days
have flown away like snow geese flying
low over a quiet pond and my arms
are empty of you and full of longing.
My autumn is a soft season when

the petals drop one by one from the tree
and the geese come to rest on the pond.
Their soft calling is like your sweet voice
when we rode our bikes and you were
ready to pull over and rest.

I gave you water and we lay there
falling on our backs into the vast sky,
falling deeply into our Hearts together
like geese going under to feed.
Then they rise. They fly away.

There is in the distance the calling,
the fleeting shadows across the Moon.
Then the silence,
the still pond,
the feather floating in it.

Bathing in the Buffalo River

The Earth is a heart
which pumps this river
like an open vein;
my daughters and I
descend from our dawn camp
to bathe
as the sun opens its eye
behind the dark mountain
and the Buffalo River runs red
in first light.

The stone-ribbed canyon
rises and falls around them
as the children plunge;
a warm breeze sighs
through the waking trees
and joyful cries go breaking
down the long stone trough,
wind and human voice
making magic morning song.

My daughters wade ashore on fire with dawn,
their lean bodies bathed in a pristine light,
their faces bright with joy.
They race to hug and hold me,
to pull me boldly into the current
which enfolds us and carries us away.

Just then
a loon sails over us
dancing in a pale haze of dawn,
bends in a blaze of feathers
to bless us with its cry,
rides heavenward on a warm draft
and glides away over the dark mountain.

We are awed into silence,
draw close to hold one another;
the Earth plays with her naked children
like wind
with flickering candles.
All of us die soon,
like the loon's brief parting call
rising over darting fish, huddled flesh,
and then falling quickly away.

And the Buffalo River holds us
as we live and die in our love for each other;
we go under,
rise again,
emerge naked from the water
and lie down on smooth stones
warmed in early morning light.

Patient vultures circle overhead;
we laugh and laugh.

For Rain Drop Who Grows Up

April morning, little one.
Sleeves bloom thin with arms,
fingers sprout. You laugh and
kiss my face, holding tight
like childhood might slip away
without you knowing,
if you did not hold me so.

April morning, little one.
We skip to breakfast singing;
you slip away from me
into adolescence
and are gone.
My God, your bed is empty,
your clothes small and unworn,

you books unopened, vacant
on your bedroom shelf.
Your breakfast is still here on the table
and you are nowhere to be seen.
I could search the wild ground of my memory,
by day calling, by night falling asleep weeping,
and still you would not be found.

April morning, little one.
I awake feeling I am not alone.
Rain falls with a wild high tone
like a small child singing.
You are a welcome guest Rain Drop.
You come and go like the seasons.
I am so pleased to see you, dear one.

Come into my house before you grow
and spend the morning here with me.
I have breakfast if you hunger,
will read to you a story from my heart.
I will not stop you when you wish to go,
but will open the door for you, bow low
and though heart calls, will not follow.

Oh my little one, it is April
and the morning will not slow
for a moment. Even now the sky is aglow
and darkness creeps closer. I know
the beat of time plays my heart like a hollow
drum Rain Drop. It is I who must go now.
Let the rain fall gently on my brow.

The Porcelain Rabbit

Little Wind was 6 when she made it
with 2 lumps for eyes on the side
of its head, one huge ear straight up
like a stick stuck in river mud,
a tail like a small fist.

I always loved it but never dreamed
that one day it would be
all I have of her, all there is
left to hold in my hands after
everything has gone wrong between us.

My daughter's heart beats in the glazed stone,
the lumpish eyes gaze fondly at me
and it whispers, Do-Do
I have always loved you.
I am tender with it,

wrap it in velvet and carry it
in my pocket when I move from
place to place as if I could save
what is fragile from breaking, what is
clearly loved from turning to stone.

Care must be given to precious things
or they disintegrate, like Virginia Woolf
who pauses at the river's edge, pockets full
of stones, and wedges her walking stick carefully
in the mud before she strides into the water;

as it closes slowly over her, she
reaches up, her white fist on the dark
wet boulder like a porcelain rabbit who
sits there trembling and alone as the
air escapes the explosion of bubbles.

It is the last thing to go under, slowly
like a man sliding a porcelain rabbit into his
pocket before he departs. He strides into
the dark, fist in his pocket
like a stick stuck in river mud.

How Little Wind Got Her Name

She was 6 when we climbed that mountain
overlooking the Salmon River,
sat there alone and quiet
deeply in love with one another.
The wind blew an owl feather
right to her feet, just like that.

　　Look Dad　she said, handing it to me,
　　Look what the little wind gave me.
And that's when she knew her name
and told me so.

What she couldn't know then was
how that moment
made me want to be a better man
to honor her.

So 8 years later
I went to live with a Master
to find out if it's possible
for a little man to act decently,
to be worthy of a gift
carried on the wind.

I found out and I lost her;
she thought I deserted her.
It's okay
because what she cannot yet know
is it's not so simple to lose a man
whose whole life is an act of gratitude
honoring an old and noble soul
who reached down for an owl feather
on a mountain in Idaho,
introduced herself,
and handed her father
his heart on a feather.

The Zanies and the Stooge

They came into this world with
a fully developed sense of humor,
both of my daughters.
As soon as they were old enough
to sit in a high chair,

we played the 'Boom-Boom' game:
they hit the tray with one hand
and I said, Boom
every time they hit it. Soon
they learned to feint

and fake me out, coming half-way
while I hollered out, Boom.
We laughed and laughed then.
All comics need a good stooge,
one who falls for the feint

every time,
the poor sucker who takes the fall
and gets the laughs.
I thank God for the Zanies.
They found the one thing

I could do well
and they put me to work:
Boom, I'd say
and their hand was
frozen in air; we laughed

until God begged for mercy.
Few are they who come into this world
with full humor;
fewer still are they who
find a willing stooge.

Alex at the Waterfall

He is 7 and as old
as they come
and one day he and his
present mother
are high over Falls Creek
when Alex gets to the overlook
and will not go close to the edge.
Why, he is asked.

Because, he says
I do not want to die
young, before my time;
I don't want to get shot,
or run over, or fall off a cliff.

I want to live my whole life and
die when I'm supposed to die,
not before.

Have you died young before,
in another time?
Yes, he said. But
I had different parents then.
You're the best parents I've
ever had,

he said
and he sat down on a rock and
he did not go over to the edge.

Old Darrell

He was too shy and gentle to last long;
that kind almost never does.
Everyone said it was awful
the way he went out:
rifle to the head
in the woods behind the Deaf School.
He was 24.

I think Old Darrell did good,
better than most maybe.
Got out
before the diabetes ate up his body
and gangrene claimed his legs
like my diabetic neighbor who is 70
and sits in his chair all day, stunned
and wondering out loud where his legs went.

I think old Darrell did good;
got out
before a woman stole his heart away
and left, tossing it easily in her hand
like a cheap rubber ball.

I think old Darrell did good;
rode out to the edge of his loneliness,
turned around in it 2, 3 times
settled in his nest behind the Deaf School
when no one could hear
the unspeakably soft cry
of a shy man;

he took apart the rifle
and laid the pieces neatly on the blanket:
brushed and oiled the trigger housing,
softly reamed the barrel with a poke,
disassembled spring and hammer;

cleaned and slowly put the world back together
with the clear and minute patience
of a man whose clock has stopped
and the tick-tock of his heart
is the only sound he's hearing
in that deaf and gentle clearing
where Darrell is transformed
into the antique hero
of the everlasting moment

as he puts in one shell only
and he looks around, not lonely,
not afraid, just
dead ready to step out of his parade.

I think old Darrell did good.

Earth

The Secret Teachings of the Forest

i. stone

Be patient.

A huge stone may wait 10,000 years without a quiver
until exactly the right moment
when it tumbles down the mountain
in an ecstasy of movement,
hurling itself into the river;
for 1,000 years more
it may stand as a monument of will,
resisting the river's roar,
its fierce tear and relentless wear, until

exactly the right opportunity,
at the peak of the thousandth winter flood,
it begins its slow deliberate pilgrimage.
Down stony bed, through swirl of mud
and floating log, over ancient Cedar root
it crushes its way to the sea.

No hurrying.

An old man comes to the snow-swollen river,
carefully lays his body beneath a Cedar tree,
gazes in wonder at the huge stone surging
just under the surface of the urgent flood.
Rooted in his calm and steady gaze
he retires from his flesh and blood.

There is no need to hurry.

The Secret Teachings of the Forest

ii. river

Be fluid.

The river flows cleanly through the trees,
always downhill, always seeking ease
of movement, the path of least resistance:
say a huge stone is hurled in its path
and for a thousand years
through melt and swell of winter storm
or burst of springtime flood,
it scarcely budges.

The river adjusts,
goes along, goes around,
has no fight with anything,
just yields ground;
it barely nudges,
parries instead of thrusts.
Slowly, the river brings
tall mountains down.

No resisting.

By the swollen river a young man sheds his clothes,
knows this freezing flood, throws himself in
at the wildest point, is mild and still, goes
far under without struggle, spins
onto a huge stone which pins and then frees him.
The flood carries him 3 miles downstream, leaves him
bruised but unbroken, on his knees, exhausted.

There is no need to resist.

The Secret Teachings of the Forest

iii. tree

Be rooted.

200 years on a gentle grassy rise,
deep-rooted Cedar guards the river;
it is undressed by winter.
Its high branches root the sky.
The Medicine man made it his ally.
He comes now, lies down there.
When young, he offered his body to the river
to test the element of surprise,
to learn the laws of attention by giving the best
he had to offer: wasting little on surmise,
he leaped into spring or winter flood, left the rest
to chance. He learned that a man is wise
who follows nothing but his heart;
a man rooted in attention is blessed;
surprise will make him fluid and humble.

No drifting.

He has come to his tree to die,
to feed the body of his ally.
His mind wants to drift
but he is strong in his heart,
has earned the gift
of attention. By fit and start
body gives in to surprise of death; he lifts
up through high branches, tumbles into the sky.

There is no need to drift.

The Secret Teachings of the Forest

iv. wolf

Be watchful.

She never had a chance;
she was hit without warning
as she loped easily down the river trail,
nose up to take the man-scent
she had smelled for miles. She never saw
the trap hidden in the deep snow
and it snapped her paw with relish
in its massive metal jaw.

No wavering.

Without hesitation she began to chew her way free.
Like a dark cloud staining a summer sky,
blood spread in the snow; she made no cry.
Within minutes tendon and bone gave way
and she began her slow crawl to safety,
dragging the bloody stump a few feet,
stopping to lick, rising again weakly.

In this way she went a mile toward her den
before she found the body by the river,
under the Cedar tree where it lay concealed.
She fed on it until she healed.
On 3 legs she scavenged then.

Now she watches, never running;
she follows her nose with unwavering intent.
Once she was a swift killing instrument;
Now she is all patient nostril cunning.

There is no need to waver.

The Secret Teachings of the Forest

v. The Wolf and the Dog

Be free.

The winter was bitter and hard so
she was starving as she struggled
on 3 legs down the river trail.

Naturally, she was surprised to see
the dog appear, so fat
and sleek of fur.

In her own way, she asked the dog
his circumstances,
how he came by his meat.

In his own way, the dog
begged the wolf to come to his home
and the wolf, who was starving, agreed.

No dependence.

When they neared the edge of the forest
she spotted the collar on the dog's neck
and in her own way asked about it.

She learned then about the men who own beasts;
she stopped; in the spring, under the giant Cedar,
they found her body by the river, starved.

There is no need to be dependent.

When Wolves Prowl The Streets

I will tell you about the time in Central Russia
in the towns along the Ob,
when people did not dare to leave their homes
except in armed groups for fear that the wolves
would attack and eat them.
They came right into the towns in large packs,
showed themselves openly and did not run away
unless they were shot at
and one of their number fell dead.
Then they would retreat, but only
just far enough to be out of range.
Livestock was slaughtered by the hundreds,
a few children in every town lost,
men and women set upon.
They lay in bed at night and heard
the scratching at their doors.
This went on for 3 months in the dead of winter,
and then they were gone; no trace,
no sign, scat, or spoor
was found by any door.

Some say the devil came
and claimed those souls which belonged to him.
Others say it was the wrath of God.
But the old ones say wolves
serve the Moon.
Sometimes it grows ravenous and must be fed.
They call this the Blood Moon;
it cultivates us the way
a farmer raises sheep,
shearing our life force.
When it grows restless, the wolves multiply;
they come for the livestock,
both 2- and 4-legged.
They howl and worry the warm meat.

They say we are given a huge dreaming brain
to keep us occupied and enthralled
while we fatten
so we never know we are being set up
until the wolves come.

How to Kill a Wolf

Go deep into the North Woods,
Canada say, where no Human is
likely to stumble over you and
lie down flat on your back

with your head back so
your throat is exposed. Lie there
very still with a knife clutched
easily in one hand by your side.

He will smell you soon enough.

Later, if he has had his fill
he will howl good meat
from one hill to the next
until the rest come for the feast,

but he will come first to make sure
he gets the best parts and he
is your boy.
He will take his time with the

circle and sniff

and he will edge and start as he
closes in on you. As much as he likes
the meats he knows Humans are bad news,
so you must not move a muscle and

barely breathe. When he is satisfied
and goes for your throat, plunge the knife
into his breast. If you miss or are too slow,
rest easy; he will be quick with you and

all is not yet lost:

your meat may be so foul it kills him;
he may die howling and laughing
over you; oh, it could go so many ways
but the best would be that you

lived a holy life, grew sweet and mild so
the big wolf falls in love with your tenderness
and he will not leave the spot where
your rot turns to dirt and he lays there

in it until he dies of longing for you.

In Her Quiet Window
(for Sweet Apple)

Her heart is in the land
and does not thrive apart from it;
like a seed in hand

she longs for dirt.
She is the wife of the apple trees
and in her long flannel shirt

she sits in the dawning window
gazing at her beloveds through the haze
of thin winter light, like a longing widow

calling for her lover to return.
Her bare limbs flash leanly as she rises
to bank the fire in a slow burn.

Her life is not subject to the treasons
of swift mood or changing style;
she lives in the seasons

and her changes are slow as
snow clouds drifting over the mountain.
She stands before the fire, bathes in its glow.

The horses call for their food
and she smiles as she dresses to feed them;
sunrise is her style, winter her mood.

The Dying Man Puts In His Garden

One more time
the holy details,
preparing the earth, thinking:
this is how they ready my grave;

hoping it will be done right
and by someone who cares for it,
the way he cares for the frail seed
he places in the moist and tender soil.

He covers it and moves on,
making neat and careful rows because
the sense is in the simple things,
the attention to the fullness

of the minutes. The seed
strains for release from its pod,
longs to catch the first glory
of the light.

The Growth of the Soil

All that can be seen comes from it,
returns.
Its perfume pleases the ordinary man
like no other
so on bended knee he gathers it in his hands,
holds it close
so he can deeply breathe it,
can feel it in his fingers.
It is the Woman
from whom he learns about all others.

We are taught to strip it naked,
to use and abuse it,
to leave it exhausted and move on;
so we do.

We drain it, leave it barren
and it dries up, wastes away,
is caught by every easy breeze
and carried off
like a badly used woman
who has no power to resist
the beckoning of strangers.

The ordinary man
serves his Beloved without complaint.
With a gentle hand
he toils for the soil
and prays that she will be well.

While all around him
she is dying of despair,
he labors and he prays.
She showers him with flowers;
she feeds him and sustains;
She endures.
This is his reward.

part iii: The Way of Attention

The Teaching

It is as old as the stones.
It came with Humans to the Earth
and it offers them a way out
of the web of sorrows
but at a price:
we must observe ourselves,
our behavior, our
inner and outer responses,
objectively. This means
without taking a personal interest
or doing anything about
the horror
which self observation uncovers:
like a bad boy with a stick
overturning a stone
and finding a mass of crawling things
beneath, but
he refrains
from stomping on them.

How the Ancient Hunting Societies Initiated a Novice

The whole village would starve
if they did not bring back meat,
so the hunters had to have
special qualities.
Lacking them,
the people perished.

The novice went through rigorous training
which placed great demands upon his
survival skills. But for his final exam
the novice was placed in a tree,
waiting there above the path
where the animals traveled.

When a Lion came stalking beneath
he jumped on the Lion's back,
a knife in each hand.
The others crouched in the bushes,
spears in hand.
If he survived,

he was one of them.

How the Huron Hunted Bear

Killing is always a trade:
if done with courage and great risk,
the spirit of the hunter is ennobled;
if not, the spirit of the hunter
is weakened and soon lost.

The Huron understood this.
Their interest was the inner life
for which you have to pay.
One of the ways they paid
was hunting bear.

One man went alone into the woods
armed with a sharp knife.
The others gave him up for lost;
if he returned,
he was a hero.

He walks until he finds bear spoor,
tracks it to the den, then
pitches stones into the den until
it comes for him.
He backs up against a man-sized tree

with the knife in his fist,
point straight out.
The bear charges and rears,
wraps man and tree in its squeeze,
impales itself on the blade.

Then it is a question of which
gives out first, man's breath
or bear's heart. The man
takes the bear's breath in his face.
If he returns,

he is a hero.

What Women Can Do When Times Get Hard

The Indians ate their dogs.
One of them, usually the Medicine man,
went to the pack,
prayed and explained the need,
then whichever one came forward
they seized it and cut its throat,
quick put a bowl beneath
to catch the blood;
mixed with herbs and things it made
a rich gravy or you could
drink it straight from the bowl,
either way it nourished you.
The children usually got the intestines,
the hunters the organ meats,
the women the shanks and marrow.
Don't think badly of them,
they did it in a sacred manner
and usually as the last choice.
Just wait until it gets so bad
you start to starve and your children
cry and their bellies get big.
Then you will call sweetly to Rover,
Come here boy,
a knife behind your back.
But don't forget the bowl;
you don't want to lose the blood.
Have the fire ready;
roasting is good, boiling better
when the meat is stringy.
Always choose a male so
you still have your supply.
When the last dog is gone call out
to the first man who happens by,
Come here baby,
and show him some thigh.

Have the fire ready and
don't forget the bowl.

The Man Who Photographed the Indians
(for Curtis & Jake)

They changed him.
At first he wore a stiff collar and tie,
carried an old newspaper he read over and over
because there was nothing else;
they thought it was part of his magic.

The Medicine man Spotted Tail came that first year
with a good horse to trade for it.
He could not believe it, a horse for a paper,
refused.

After a time, Spotted Tail came again:
two horses for his paper.
It made him laugh hysterically.
He could not understand it, was embarrassed,
refused.

The third time Spotted Tail came:
3 horses, a fringed and beaded jacket, a buffalo robe;
by then he knew enough
to take one horse, the jacket.
Spotted Tail grew famous for the paper.

They befriended him,
posed with their hearts in their eyes.
By then he knew enough
not to ask them to smile.

When he finally left for Seattle,
he knew enough not to look back.
He wore the jacket to his exhibits,
longed to tell what he had seen
but stayed quiet, trusted the photos.

By then he knew enough
to let his heart be in his eyes,
to give everything he had for magic.
They buried him in the jacket.

How the Iroquois Dealt With Their Wayward Sons
(for Muldoon)

Each spring at gelding time,
the Iroquois men
gathered together the bad boys,
those whose sap was boiling
and overflowing without control.

They took them among the horses,
selecting those who would not
respond to proper training
to be gelded.
They yelled at the horse,
You will not do as you're told,
and then they weeded them out.

It was the task of the bad boys
to take a piece of wet rawhide,
one boy on each end, and
loop it around the horse's balls,
drawing it tight while the horse
was held down by strong men as
another of the boys cut and sliced,
usually with a sharp stone or
a finely honed clam shell
from one of the Great Lakes.

At the end of this ritual
the men would roast their spoils
and eat with relish. Often
the young boys would refrain.
The Iroquois
never had any trouble
with their sons.

The Battle Axe
(for Snake & Little Horse)

As soon as the boy was born
the men went into the woods
with the heavy worked stone in hand
and they selected a Hickory tree.
Choosing one strong green limb
they split it a little ways
from the trunk. Then
they drove wedges into the split

carefully

until it was just wide enough
to take the stone.
Removing the wedges, they wrapped
on either side of the stone
with wet rawhide strips
that drew tight as they dried.

Then they left it,
going back with the boy
every now and then
to see how it grew.

In his fourteenth year
he came with the men
to cut the limb at the trunk.
The stone was part of the tree,
immovable, heavy as thunder.

This was his axe.

At first it was too much for him,
required more muscle to wield
with the necessary grace
to kill a man.
He had to grow into it
the way a green stone grows into wood.

It taught him patience,
when to give and
how to take away;

it taught respect for the tool
and for the job
it was made to do.

The Protocol of the Water Hole

The Gabra are a desert tribe.
They live for water and the camel
is their means of finding it;
camels smell water
the way a dog smells bear.
They move from water hole to hole
and their lives depend
on doing it right.

This means exact precision
when they near a hole.
Each driver is responsible
for the movement of his camel:
its head is muffled,
it is brought to its knees,
staked down and fed while
one by one they are led to the hole.

If one driver fails
to hold his camel
all is lost.
The camels will stampede,
some will be killed
or badly injured
and the hole poisoned
by pee and shit.

If there is a stampede,
the responsible driver is stripped bare,
blinded, and set out in the desert.
For the Gabra
there is no second chance;
there is mastery of the beast
or there is the dark wandering,
the hot sand searing the naked soles.

There Are Some Among Us Who Will
Do Anything For Truth

Bodhidharma walked barefoot to China
with his shoes tied on top of his head
after he was enlightened living with Buddha.
When he got to the emperor's palace and saw
that the wisest men in the court were all fools
he went to the edge of town and sat facing
the Great Wall and refused to turn around until
someone with some sense showed up and
they had better be able to prove it.
8 years he sat there, winter and summer.
Hundreds came but he did not turn.

One day a voice said, If you do not turn
and teach me I will cut my hand off.
When he did not turn, a bloody stump
was flung at his feet. He turned.
What took you so long, he said.
I have been waiting.
And he took his first disciple.

Men like that, choose the one
standing with only one hand or
the one sitting down with 3,
are rare in any age but in our own
they are here, they can be found.
I have seen them and lived among them.
In this day and age they
do not require anything so dramatic;
your life will do.

Go now. But take the
sharpest axe you can find with you
in case I am wrong.
You do not want to go there
with a dull blade.

Heaven

When I raised up and looked around I saw
I was surrounded by people in heavy grey
wool overcoats, stamping their feet and beating
their arms about their ribs to stay warm,
their collective breath hanging like a coroner's
sheet over their heads.

It's cold, I said, where is the heat?
One of them turned and glared at me.
Go to hell if you want heat,
he said. There they are naked and
shovel coal into the great furnace
that heats the worlds and they
never rest.
What do you do here? I asked.
He stared at me. We stand and wait
until it is our time to go back and
do it all over again, he said.

There was a clatter of hooves and men
on white horses rode roughly through
the crowd, fur parkas protecting them
from the cold. All rushed forward
to block their way, clamoring
and beseeching them in an awful din.
The riders used heavy clubs to knock
certain ones hard on the head.
They fell as if dead and those
nearby rushed to take their coats.
When they did, the coats were empty.

Where did they go? I asked one who was
near me. She smiled. They have gone back
to do it all over again, she said.
The Enlightened Ones come down from the
Hill Station where they live in the temples
to select those whose time has come.

How do they choose? I asked, scared.
No one knows, she said. We just stand
here in the cold and wait. Here,
she said,
and handed me a heavy coat she had
picked up off the ground.

A Parade for Sonny Liston

I have spent the night pursued by inner demons
when I think of Sonny Liston the boxer now dead,
a man pursued by real demons as well as those

of his own devising. When Sonny beat Floyd Patterson,
another one who knew about demons, that first time
a light went on for just a moment in his life. After

years in prison, strike busting for mobsters, a life
of petty crime and violence, he flew back to Philadelphia
on top of the world in which he was the champion.

On that flight, Sonny sat with another old fighter
and he talked about his vision, how he would
make black folks proud the way Joe Louis did.

Sonny said that when the plane landed and he
spoke to the crowds who would be there to cheer,
he would talk about hope and courage to them

so they would have someone to look up to.
It was his shining moment and when he
got off that plane and there was no one there

to cheer him
it broke Sonny Liston's heart.
It proved to him he was no good and he

never doubted that again, though he doubted
everything else. This poem is Sonny's parade.
3 cheers for Sonny Liston, champion of the world,

a man like us full of doubt and sorrow,
a man with a vision who did not understand that
once you see the vision you've got to follow it

to the end, even if
no one shows up to cheer and
you wind up speaking to the wind.

Me and Ginsberg Read in Hot Springs

They came by the hundreds to hear us read.
Well, mainly they came to hear old Allen but
since I was up before him, they came
to hear us read.
Young and old alike, they cheered
and they laughed when I read and then
they stood and applauded when I finished.
Then Allen got up and he read poems
about his asshole which is well loved
among some of the famous poets and he
read poems in praise of oral sex
and that's when the old people got up
and left in droves, while the young
cheered wildly and laughed.
One old woman grabbed me
on her way out. You're ten times
the poet he is honey, she hissed
and her old rheumy friends all
nodded and smiled at me.
Ahh, vast public acceptance at last;
they like my poems
better than Ginsberg's
asshole.

The Headlines Will Draw A Brief Crowd

The governor of the state where I live
got elected president and that is
very bad news
for the Buffalo River, the Ozark
and Ouichita Mountains; the
Little Missouri Falls.
The tourists will be coming next.
Soon I will drive
to Copperhead Pool and a big mobile home
with Jersey plates will be there
and a woman will scream at the kids,
Watch out for snakes down there, they
don't call this Copperhead Pool
for nothing. And her daughter
will play the jambox loud and her
husband and brother will throw beer bottles
into the bushes and laugh and yell out
when another one smashes against a tree.
But Arkansas will take care of them quickly
when they find out it is
hotter than the outskirts of hell and
there is nothing to do here
but walk and sit and look at the glory.
By the second day the kids will
start to whine and they will soon
move out to Branson, Missouri or over to
Opryland in Tennessee.
And if that doesn't get them
the other will: they
do not call it Copperhead Pool
for nothing.

Bulletin: Red Hawk Is Not A Real Indian

The Guardians of Racial Purity are mad as hell
about my name, too color blind to see
I am a dying breed: the genuine phony Indian;
there are damn few of us left
and most of them are dead.
I come from pure drunken Anglo stock.
The name came from my Guru who
did not give a damn what you
or anyone else thought about me,

he just meant to stick me with a heavy load,
one that would give me trouble
and make me build some inner muscle
just to lug it around. It has.
Nope, I'm just another sorry white boy
with a good attitude, but a funny thing
happened to me on the way to the Phony Farm:
I met Good Horse Nation, a phony like me,
a half-breed whose only care was that

I loved the Earth and was willing to
die repeatedly for Her in the Sweat Lodge
while he piled on the stones, sang and smiled
as one after another we fell over in the dirt and
from that Holy dust some damn good men and women
stood naked and steady in the heart like stones
which have passed through the hottest fire.
He showed us how to build the Willow lodge
which had broken me down like

childbirth breaks down a good woman,
then he blessed my phony white heart and
sent me off like my Guru to go it alone.
So don't come to me with your theories
about the way things ought to be.
All that shows is you think you know something.
Big deal.
None of us knows anything
except we live in a Holy Mystery:

all IT cares about is,
Are you ready to bear the wound of love
without a whimper, and
Are you ready to lend a hand.
So soon we will be dead;
our only hope is that we can behave as
One Spirit dressed in a frail skin of Light,
warm, forgiving, and Humanly beautiful,
holding one another in the dying of the Light.

Epilogue: What I Would Tell Young Boys

What I Would Tell Young Boys

Every chance you get
watch the women, especially
the old ones and the mothers
with their children.
They enliven the soul and ground it
in the sweet soil of the heart.

Bond with them.
It is the only thing that can save you
from the madness: absolute power
has corrupted men absolutely;
it is believed 700,000 women in the U.S.
are raped each year. Half don't tell.
Of those who tell, half are humiliated
and made to feel they are at fault.

You will be told it is your duty to
whip your children and make war.
I tell you bonding with women
is your duty and your only hope.
Surrender to them, serve them,
wash their feet and thank them
for allowing one who has strayed
to come into their gentle company.

Waiting for his star to rise in the firmament,
praying for his heart to catch fire and shine,
a man carries water to bathe
the women and children;
he holds, lifts, and turns
the old and the dying;
he forgets himself completely.
He is revered in the company of women

because he is tender hearted and kind,
a man who can be trusted
and for whom they have no fear.
He who bonds with women
will be shown the content of heaven.
The truly damned, those turned out
of heaven, are they who strike fear
in the hearts of women and children.